What Is
the Stanley Cup?

What Is
the Stanley Cup?

by Gail Herman

illustrated by Gregory Copeland

Penguin Workshop

For Mike, Ryan, and Liam G.—GC

PENGUIN WORKSHOP
An Imprint of Penguin Random House LLC, New York

Copyright © 2019 by Penguin Random House LLC. All rights reserved. Published by Penguin Workshop, an imprint of Penguin Random House LLC, New York. PENGUIN and PENGUIN WORKSHOP are trademarks of Penguin Books Ltd. WHO HQ & Design is a registered trademark of Penguin Random House LLC. Printed in the USA.

Visit us online at www.penguinrandomhouse.com.

Library of Congress Cataloging-in-Publication Data is available upon request.

ISBN 9781524786472 (paperback)   10 9 8 7
ISBN 9781524786489 (library binding)   10 9 8 7 6 5 4 3 2 1

Contents

What Is the Stanley Cup?

Each June, a series of hockey games ends by crowning a championship team. The winner is the number one team in the United States and Canada, and perhaps the world.

The Stanley Cup is considered the most difficult sports championship to win, with thirty-one teams in the National Hockey League, sixteen teams in the playoffs, and three rounds of best-of-seven-games series before the finals.

Whew!

The prize is the Stanley Cup itself—the oldest and most famous sports trophy in the world. Its origins go back more than a hundred years. Thousands of fans have lined up around the world just to catch a glimpse of it.

After the final buzzer of the final game, the

captain of the winning team is presented with the Cup. He lifts it high overhead. He circles the rink, his teammates following in a parade. In turn, they each take a lap with the prize.

Some players kiss it. Some cry. And some are surprised by its weight. (It weighs 34½ pounds.)

All these players know they hold history in their hands. The same "Presentation Cup," topped with a copy of the original trophy's bowl, has been awarded for more than fifty years.

Thousands of names are engraved in the bowl and on its bands—names of winning teams from the 1890s and, later, player, coach, and staff-member names.

Some teams listed—like the Vancouver Millionaires and the Montreal Wanderers—haven't been around for almost a century.

Since 1995, the trophy travels the globe for about three hundred days each year. (The rest of the time, it's on display at the Hockey Hall of

The Montreal Wanderers, 1905

Fame in Toronto, Ontario.) Each championship team member spends a day with "Stanley."

It's been to hometowns in the United States and Canada, plus Russia, the Czech Republic, Sweden, Finland, and even the tropical Bahamas. It's been used as a bowl for popcorn, ice cream,

cereal, and dog food. And two babies have been christened in it.

It's the stuff of tradition and legend. And it all started with one man: a British lord, Frederick Arthur Stanley.

CHAPTER 1
The Start of It All

Ice hockey has roots in ball-and-stick games, dating back to the earliest civilizations. In colder climates, people played these sports on frozen ponds, eventually on skates. Canada, though, is considered the true birthplace of hockey, combining these games and First Nations

(Canadian indigenous people) traditions. In Montreal, James Creighton, the "Father of Organized Hockey," introduced the first real rules, holding an "official" hockey game indoors—using a puck instead of a ball—in 1875.

During the sport's early years, players didn't wear helmets, padding, or goalie masks. They stayed on the ice every second of the game. There were no nets, just posts hammered into the ice.

In June 1888, Lord Frederick Arthur Stanley and his family arrived in Canada. Queen Victoria of England had named him governor-general. At the time, Canada was a "dominion"—or territory—of England. The governor-general was appointed by the British king or queen to govern Canada.

Lord Stanley and his wife, Constance

Canadian Geography

Canada is the second-largest country in the world. Its ten provinces function in a similar way as states in the United States, and its three territories have slightly different rules of government.

Today, hockey is considered the national pastime of Canada. It's part of the nation's culture and identity.

Provinces, territories, and major hockey cities in Canada

None of the Stanleys knew about hockey. But Lord Stanley and his eight children loved sports. After seeing a game in Montreal, they were hooked. Two of the Stanley brothers formed a team of seven players, the standard number back then. They traveled in their father's private train to play other teams. Throughout the country, people took notice. This was the important governor-general's family!

The game became popular in northern US cities, too. Meanwhile, more leagues formed.

In time, Lord Stanley's children wanted to hold a championship; one winner named from among all the different leagues. Lord Stanley donated a silver punch bowl to use for the trophy. So the Stanley Cup isn't really a "cup" at all.

Trophy Trivia

Since 1958, the Stanley Cup has had five bands below its bowl, filled with champions' names. Every twelve or thirteen years, the oldest band is taken off and displayed in the Hockey Hall of Fame, while the other four are moved up, and a blank band is added for new winners. Through the years, there have been many typos. When the Bruins won the title in 1972, *Boston* was spelled *BQSTQN*. The 1980–81 New York Islanders' name was written as *ILANDERS*. The *Leafs* in Toronto Maple Leafs was spelled *LEAES* in 1963. Hall of Fame goaltender Jacques Plante won the Stanley Cup six times between 1953 and 1960. His name is spelled five different ways. And there have been other problems: In 1984, the Oilers' owner included his dad's name on the list. It was later crossed out.

According to Lord Stanley's wishes, the trophy was a "challenge cup." What did that mean?

Teams had two ways to win the trophy. One way was simple enough. A team just had to be in the same league as the last champions and finish first in standings, beating out the reigning Cup-holder.

Then there was the "challenge" way. To get the Cup, teams from different leagues had to challenge the championship team to a game or series of games. And of course, the challenger had to win. Challenges could come any time—before, during, or after the hockey season. And there were no limits on how many could be issued. (Sometimes there'd be five Stanley Cup contests in one season!)

Sound confusing? Well, things were about to get even more complicated.

CHAPTER 2
Who's Up for the Challenge?: 1893–1913

Lord Stanley named a committee—with members called trustees—to be in charge of the Stanley Cup. In 1893, the first year of the Cup, the trophy went to the best team in the best league: the Montreal Hockey Club. The team had

The Montreal Hockey Club with the first Stanley Cup, 1893

the first true hockey star, Haviland Routh, who scored twelve goals in seven games.

The trophy was engraved with "Montreal AAA." But Routh and his teammates turned it down. Their league name was the Montreal Amateur Athletic Association. It was not their team name. To the players, it didn't make sense. Plus, they hadn't been invited to the official presentation and didn't even know, really, what the trophy was about.

The next year, the club came out on top again. This time, the *team* had the trophy engraved, saying simply, "Montreal 1894."

It seemed a sure bet that the Montreal Hockey Club would win again. But they were out of the running after dropping to second place in their league. Instead, the number one team, called the Montreal Victorias, won the title, despite not even playing one challenge game. Weird rules, right?

In fact, the trustees seemed to be making up

Montreal Victorias, 1895

rules as they went. Sometimes the championship was decided by just one game. Sometimes it was the best of three. And sometimes the series was two games, with the scores combined.

Adding to the confusion, the Montreal "Vics" shared a name with the Winnipeg Victorias. Before the teams faced each other for the Cup in 1896, fans gathered at the Winnipeg train station to see *their* Vics off. At the Valentine's Day game, the crowd sang for hours: "Hobble gobble, razzle dazzle, sis boom bah. Victoria, Victories, rah, rah, rah."

This was in the days before telephones, radio, and TV. Fans were getting their news by telegraph. Back in Winnipeg, hundreds gathered outside hotels to hear play-by-play bulletins read out loud. Then came the news. Winnipeg had won, 2–0.

An even larger crowd gathered at the station when the team returned. Cheering loudly, they followed the players into town. From then on, having a Stanley Cup parade became a tradition.

Just ten months later, Montreal won back the Cup. And by 1903, there'd be a new team to beat: the Ottawa Hockey Club. The team's official name was the Senators, the same as the modern-day one. But everybody called them the Silver Seven. The seven players had all received a bonus for their first championship, a nugget of silver. And the nickname stuck.

The rough-and-ready Silver Seven held on to their title through ten challenges. Their number one player was "One-Eyed" Frank McGee. After a hit in a hockey game years earlier, he'd lost the sight in his left eye. Even half blind, McGee kept scoring and never said no to a fight.

"One-Eyed" Frank McGee

All the team's players fought hard, some viciously. They used the "Ottawa hook"— wrapping their hockey sticks around an opponent's neck. After a challenge game against the Toronto Marlboros, one newspaper headline read: "Marlboros Beaten by Ottawa. But Not at Hockey."

But the Silver Seven's most famous match came in 1905, when a little-known team from the remote north issued a challenge. The Dawson City team called themselves the Nuggets; they came from Gold Rush territory, the Yukon.

Gold Rush in the Yukon

A gold rush is a rush for gold, with prospectors hurrying across great distances to seek their fortunes. In 1896, three friends discovered a gold nugget in a creek by the Klondike River. In days, the area swarmed with newcomers. But the real rush came in July 1897, when a ship carrying miners—and more than a ton of gold—docked in

Seattle. Immediately, tens of thousands of people traveled from around the world to the Yukon, a region of Canada bordering Alaska and the Arctic Ocean. Along the dangerous route, people were murdered, fell ill, starved to death, and were killed in avalanches. Less than one-third even made it to Dawson City, the mining base. And only about four thousand people found any gold at all. When news came of another gold rush, most moved on.

The once-bustling Dawson City was in the middle of nowhere. Its team played hockey mostly to pass the time. Their goalie was only seventeen, still to this day the youngest player to compete for the Cup. The question was, could the Nuggets even arrive at the matches in time? To reach Ottawa, they had to travel almost four thousand miles.

The team went by dogsled and bicycle, foot and stagecoach, boat and train. They faced snow and bitter cold.

Finally, after a month-long trip, they arrived in Ottawa. It was just two days before the first game. The players barely had time to sleep, much less practice. They lost 9–2. But Dawson City had held One-Eyed McGee to one goal.

What is the big deal about McGee? the Nuggets players asked around town. In the next game, the Nuggets found out. McGee scored fourteen times in a 23–2 rout, a scoring record to this day.

CHAPTER 3
Big Changes: 1906–1916

The next year brought one major change to Canadian hockey leagues. Up until the 1905–06 season, hockey players had been amateurs; they weren't paid. But the Stanley Cup kept making news. Competition grew stronger. Teams wanted to get the best talent.

And they were willing to pay. The Cup turned professional. Some leagues disbanded. New ones formed, including the National Hockey Association, with teams like the Montreal Wanderers and the Montreal Canadiens.

The Canadiens

Founded in 1909, the Montreal Canadiens are the only National Hocky League (NHL) team older than the modern-day pro hockey league itself. The team has had rosters of all-time greats, starting with "the Babe Ruth of Hockey," Howie Morenz (1923–37), along with Jean Beliveau, winner of the NHL Lifetime Achievement Award (1950–71). As of 2018, the Canadiens have won more titles (twenty-four) than any other NHL team and are the only ones to win the Cup five times in a row.

Howie Morenz and Jean Beliveau

The Wanderers' captain and main defender, Lester Patrick, led his team to two titles. At one point, Lester made more money than the prime minister of Canada. Then Lester and his brother, Frank, another talented player, moved west to British Columbia. They wanted to run a lumber business. They thought their hockey days were over.

They were wrong.

Lester and Frank Patrick

In 1911, after selling the company, the brothers started a league. The new Pacific Coast Hockey Association (the PCHA) would soon have hockey clubs in the northwest United States as well as in Canada.

The Patricks played and coached, using new rules on rinks with artificial ice and blue lines. Lester Patrick had another idea, too: "to have a series of games, such as the World Series, to decide the championship."

The very next season, the Patricks' league—in the west—signed an agreement with the NHA—in the east: The Stanley Cup would be between these two leagues and no others. Eventually, another western league formed, and a west coast playoff format was established. But there'd still be only one championship series at the end of every season, featuring the top team from each coast. For all intents and purposes, the challenge era was over.

In 1914, "the World Series of Hockey" began. About the same time, a devastating worldwide event was taking place: World War I broke out that summer. Canada joined the conflict as soon as England declared war against Germany. (The United States remained out of the war until 1917.) With so many Canadian hockey players joining the military, the leagues struggled.

Still, teams played on. They had names like the Vancouver Millionaires, the Quebec Bulldogs, the Spokane Canaries, and from Portland, Oregon, the Rosebuds.

In 1916, the Rosebuds made it to the Cup, the first American team to do so. (However, there actually was only one US player on the team.) Nicknamed the Uncle Sams, they were up against the Canadiens.

Where Are They From?

In the early 1900s, most every hockey player was Canadian. In the 1917–18 season, for instance, there were forty players from Canada and only three from the United States. But as more American teams formed, the number of US-born players increased.

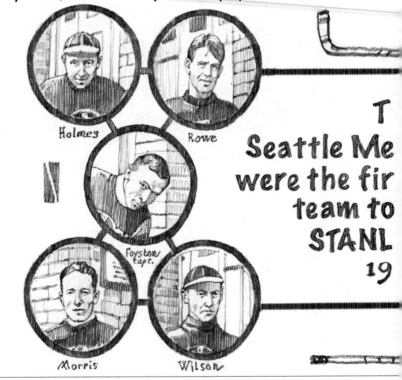

Holmes

Rowe

Foyston capt.

Morris

Wilson

T
Seattle Me
were the fir
team to
STANL
19

Eventually, players from around the world signed up for the NHL, too. In the 2015–16 season, the number of Canadians dropped to just below 50 percent of players for the first time in history—24 percent were from the United States, followed by smaller groups from Sweden, Finland, Russia, and the Czech Republic.

he tropolitans
st American
win the
EY CUP
17

Carpenter   Walker
Muldoon Mgr.
Rickey   Riley

All the games were played in Montreal to save time and money. After the first two, the series was tied 1–1. In Game 3, the play was hard and rough. Canadiens star Éduoard "Newsy" Lalonde was thrown out for fighting. After the call, both team benches emptied and the first brawl in Stanley Cup history began. People in the stands joined the skirmish, too.

Finally, the chief of police arrived. He threatened to throw both teams in jail. So fans and players settled down, and Montreal ended up taking the game, 6–3. But it all came down to the fifth and last game.

With about seven minutes left, the score was tied 1–1. Montreal goalie Georges Vezina made a save, and Lalonde got the rebound. In a surprise move, the high-scorer left the puck behind the net. A Montreal defender, Goldie Prodgers, picked it up and raced down the ice. He faked out the Rosebud goalie, slipping the puck into the net.

Goldie Prodgers

The Canadiens had won their first Stanley Cup!

The next year, a different American team made it to the championship: the Seattle, Washington, Metropolitans. They took the series in four games and became the first official US winners.

Less than two weeks later, on April 6, 1917, the United States entered the war, fighting alongside Canada, England, and France. Game attendance shrank even more. The NHA fell apart. There was talk of stopping play.

Instead, NHA owners founded the NHL. And the Stanley Cup kept going.

CHAPTER 4
The NHL Takes Over: 1917–1928

World War I finally ended on November 11, 1918. However, an even deadlier worldwide disaster struck—the Spanish flu. The epidemic didn't end until the summer of 1919. An estimated twenty to fifty million people died.

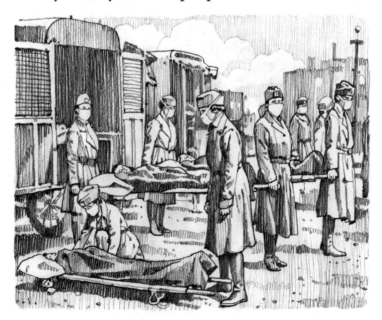

The March 1919 final of the Stanley Cup still took place. The Metropolitans and the Canadiens had a championship rematch in Seattle.

Going into Game 4, Seattle was ahead two games to one. After regulation and two overtime periods, the score was tied. Unsure what to do, officials blew the final whistle—the first Stanley Cup game to end in a draw.

Game 5 went into overtime, too. But the Canadiens squeaked out a win. However, by the end, Joe Hall and other Montreal players were slowing down. Fans just thought they were tired. Nobody thought the players were sick.

The morning of the deciding game, three Canadiens ran fevers. Hall's temperature rose to over 105 degrees. He and another player were sent to the hospital. They had the flu! The Canadiens couldn't field a team. They forfeited.

Seattle could have taken the Cup and been declared champions. They refused because they were good sports. So the series was canceled. No winner was crowned. Sadly, Hall died days later. Five years after that, the Seattle team disbanded. Other western teams folded, too.

Joe Hall

Even though now hockey was much more popular than ever, the focus wasn't on the west. It was on the east and the growing NHL. The NHL's first American team, the Boston Bruins, came on board for the 1924–25 season, followed by the New York Rangers, the Chicago Black Hawks (the name was changed to one word, Blackhawks, in 1986), and the team that would become the Detroit Red Wings.

By the 1926–27 season, the NHL had ten teams in the United States and Canada. In fact, it was the only league left. All western pro leagues had disbanded. The NHL was large enough to have divisions and playoffs. And the Stanley Cup was its trophy.

In one of the first Stanley Cup series of the NHL era, the Rangers faced the Montreal Maroons. The games started on April 5, 1928; all were held in Montreal. (That was because the Rangers' home arena was Madison Square Garden, and at that time every year, the circus took over the Garden.)

The Rangers' coach was Lester Patrick. He was already a legend in Montreal after playing for the Wanderers. How would he fare in this series? Patrick's team lost the first game, 2–0. The second game was a tense, scoreless match. To make matters worse, Ranger goalie Lorne Chabot was hit in the eye.

The New York team, without a backup, had no goalie. But the Maroons refused to allow a professional goalie, watching the game in the stands, to step in. However, they agreed to another substitute: Lester Patrick. Patrick was forty-four years old. He had been retired for six years. He'd never even played goalie in a

Lester Patrick

real game! But he stuffed socks into Chabot's large skates so they'd fit and went out onto the ice. Patrick dove and flopped. He dropped to his knees. He stopped puck after puck. Meanwhile, the Rangers scored. They were up 1–0. Could Patrick keep the shutout? There were only five minutes left in the game. Maroon Nels Stewart trapped a rebound in front of the net. He faked a shot. Patrick tried to make the save. But he moved the wrong way. The puck went in the other side.

The game went into overtime. Somehow, Patrick kept the Maroons to that one goal, while Frank Boucher netted another for the Rangers. The series was tied. For the next three games, the Rangers were allowed to use a professional goalie.

Inspired by its fearless coach, the team worked harder than ever. In the fifth game, Boucher scored both goals in a 2–1 victory, and the Rangers took the title. To celebrate, the Cup was displayed in the window of Cartier, a famous—and famously expensive!—jewelry store in New York City. It seemed a fitting place. During the "Roaring Twenties," people had been spending money freely. But the good times were drawing to a close.

CHAPTER 5
Tough Times: 1929–1941

Late 1929 brought the Great Depression, an economic crisis. Millions of people lost their jobs and their homes.

Men building shacks during the Great Depression

Hockey fans, along with everyone else, had less money to spend. They stopped going to games. As the Depression wore on, teams folded. Even big-name teams like the Ottawa Senators didn't last. The remaining teams needed big wins to keep their fans coming.

They needed the Stanley Cup.

In 1934, the Red Wings made it to the finals, only to lose to Chicago. In 1936, they were back in the playoffs. The problem: They faced defending champs, the Montreal Maroons. It was the first game of what was now a best-of-five series. The face-off was at 8:30 p.m. It could have ended by ten. But after three periods, the score was 0–0. The game went into overtime. One overtime period passed, then two and three. Hours went by. It was after 2:00 a.m. now, and the teams were in their sixth overtime. Detroit goalie Normie Smith had stopped ninety shots. Lorne Chabot, now with the Maroons, had stopped fewer, sixty-six.

Normie Smith

Would the Maroons keep pounding the net? Eventually scoring to win?

At 2:25 a.m., the youngest player on the ice that night, rookie Red Wing Modere Fernand "Mud" Bruneteau, got hold of the puck. In front of the goal, he swung his stick—hard. The puck flew over Chabot's foot, into the net. "It was the funniest thing," Bruneteau said later. "The puck just stuck 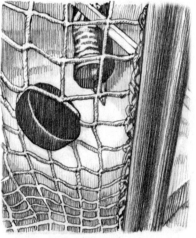 there in the twine." It never fell down. The Red Wings took the game, the longest game in Stanley Cup playoff history, and swept the series. They went on to beat the Toronto Maple Leafs in the finals and won again in 1937. But there was no three-peat. In 1938, the Red Wings didn't even make the playoffs.

The very next year, war was brewing once again in Europe. In September 1939, England and France declared war on Germany. Canada quickly followed their lead, while the United States waited to decide if it would join the conflict overseas. With an increase in factory production and jobs, World War II ended the long Depression.

But there was no cause for celebration. Too many young men were fighting and dying.

The NHL carried on as best it could. That March, in 1940, the Maple Leafs and the Rangers reached the finals. One team hailed from Toronto, a city in a country at war. The other team was based in the United States, a country, for the moment, not taking part in the fighting. The players felt the difference.

In Toronto, Canadian soldiers in uniform were everywhere. At the Leafs' arena, Toronto fans screamed their hearts out every time their team scored. When the Rangers scored, the place fell silent. Still, the Rangers pulled out a Cup win in six games.

It turned into a double celebration. The company that owned Madison Square Garden and the Rangers had just finished paying for the arena. So company officers tossed official papers about the bank loan into the Cup. They set the papers

on fire. It was their way of proclaiming their purchase of Madison Square Garden. But the trophy burned a bit, too.

It was the cause, some said, of a Stanley Cup curse.

CHAPTER 6
The Original Six: 1942–1967

In early December 1941, the United States entered the war, joining Canada and England. More and more players left the NHL for the military.

Syl Apps, former member of the Maple Leafs

By the 1942–43 season, there were six teams left. Canada had only two teams, the Canadiens and the Maple Leafs. The United States had four: the Bruins, Rangers, Red Wings, and Black Hawks. Later, they'd be called the "Original Six." But back then, fans feared even these teams couldn't last.

But a small league brought more intense matchups. Stronger rivalries. People flocked to games. And in Canada especially, hockey proved to be an escape from the war. In 1942, the Maple Leafs faced the Red Wings. They were favored to win. But Detroit took the first three games— easily. The Toronto goalie admitted, "They're unbeatable." Detroit needed one more game to win the Cup. And the team would be playing at home. It seemed like a shoo-in.

In a last-ditch effort, the Toronto coach changed the lineup. He benched his top scorer and replaced him with a substitute player, Don Metz. It was a smart move. Toronto managed to tie the score, 3–3. Then Metz set up his older brother, Nick, for the winning goal. And that was it. Toronto won.

Don Metz

As soon as the final whistle blew, the Detroit coach raced across the rink. Angry about calls and penalties, he had it out with the ref. Detroit fans joined the protest, tossing papers, peanuts, and a shoe onto the ice. The Detroit coach was suspended for the series. Could the Red Wings win one more game without him?

No!

Toronto took the next three games—helped along by Don Metz and his Game 5 hat trick. A hat trick is when a player scores three goals in a game. It's still the greatest comeback in Cup-final history.

While the war raged on, teams filled their rosters with players too old and too young to serve in the armed forces. Sometimes they signed players who had failed their army physicals. That included Maurice "Rocket" Richard. (You say his last name the French way, REE-shar.) Richard

had a history of broken bones from playing junior hockey and was rejected for military service. The NHL was worried about Richard getting injured. Was he strong enough to play professional hockey?

Maurice Richard

Sure enough, in his very first season as a Canadien, he broke his ankle and wound up playing just sixteen games out of fifty.

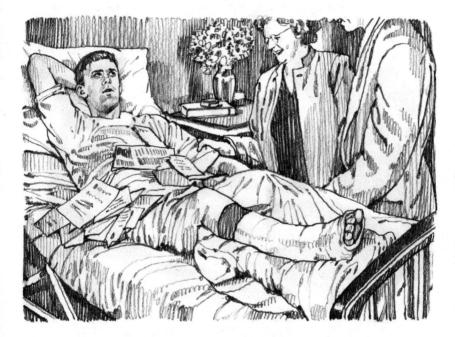

But in his second year, the 1943–44 season, Richard came back with a vengeance. He scored goal after goal. Could he keep it up for the playoffs? The semifinals against Toronto would be the test.

In the first game, Richard couldn't score. The Canadiens lost. The second game started the same way. Richard was so closely defended, he didn't take one shot. At the end of the first period, the score was 0–0. But going into the second period, Richard got the puck. He deked—faked out—the goalie, then took a quick shot. Just like that, the score was 1–0. Seconds later, Richard scored again . . . and again. By the end of the game, he held an NHL playoff record.

Newspaper headlines read: "Richard 5, Toronto 1."

The war ended in September 1945. Pro hockey players were slowly but surely returning to the game. Many thought this spelled the end of Rocket Richard's success. He'd be facing stronger, tougher competition.

It didn't matter.

In 1952, in the second period of Game 7 of the semifinals against Boston, Richard was hit in the face by a stick. He fell to the ice, unconscious. Blood streamed down his face. By the third period, he was stitched up and back in the rink. He carried the puck from end to end, dodging defenders left and right to blast a goal.

Called one of the greatest goals ever, it clinched the game and won the series. Richard was the backbone of the Canadiens. He later led the team to five straight championships from 1956 to 1960.

But in 1952, after beating Boston, the Canadiens lost the Cup to the Red Wings and their offensive star, Gordie Howe. Nicknamed "Mr. Hockey," Howe resembled Richard. He was a larger-than-life player. The Wings won championship after championship, helped by Howe's famous scoring line, the "Production Line."

Richard and Howe were legends. But it was the Toronto Maple Leafs who won four Cups in six years. *And* they had the final win in the Original Six era.

The NHL was about to expand.

Maple Leafs captain George Armstrong (left) and Harold Ballard, one of the team's owners, ride with the Stanley Cup during the championship celebration, 1967.

Right Wing Rivals

Maurice Richard (1921–2000)

The Rocket spent his entire life in Montreal. The oldest of eight children, Richard grew up in a rough city neighborhood and started playing street hockey at age four. He trained to be a machinist, like his dad, but his life was always hockey. At twenty-one, he joined the Canadiens, becoming the first hockey player ever to score fifty goals in fifty games. He retired after eighteen years with the team, eight championship titles, and an NHL scoring record. When he died at age seventy-eight, 115,000 people paid their respects at the Canadiens arena.

Gordie Howe (1928–2016)

Like Richard, "Mr. Hockey" grew up poor. He was raised in Saskatoon, Saskatchewan, the fifth of nine children. Howe got his first pair of used skates at age five. By age fifteen he was invited to professional

Maurice Richard (right) shakes hands with Gordie Howe.

training camps. At seventeen he joined a minor league team, and at eighteen he was playing for the Red Wings. During a game in 1950, Howe fractured his skull. Doctors thought he wouldn't survive. The very next season, he was the league's top scorer. At forty-three, Howe retired with records for goals, assists, and total points. But he came back to play alongside his sons, ending his career with the NHL's Hartford Whalers at age fifty-two, one of the oldest athletes ever to play a major league sport.

CHAPTER 7
More Teams, More Excitement: 1968–1979

Hockey sticks were curved. Goalies wore masks. Substitutions were frequent. For the 1967–68 season, the NHL swelled to twelve teams, adding the Los Angeles Kings, the Pittsburgh Penguins, and others—six in all, known as expansion teams. By then the game had changed. Even

so, the Boston Bruins still weren't winning championships.

The team went eight straight years without making the playoffs. Then, in 1968, they were knocked out in the first round. They reached the second round the next year—and lost. But in the 1970 semifinals, they swept the Black Hawks, silencing Bobby Hull, the left winger said to have a 119-mile-per-hour shot. One player made the difference: hockey great Bobby Orr— the only defender ever to win the scoring title.

Bobby Orr

The Bruins began the finals with a likely sweep, too. They had near-blowout wins in the first three games. But in Game 4, the St. Louis Blues matched them goal for goal. At the end of regulation, it was 3–3.

Seconds into overtime, Orr skated to the net, ready for a return pass. He got the puck and gave it a tap. Just then, a defender knocked him high into the air. But Orr knew he'd already scored. In mid-flight, he spread his arms in victory, shouting and smiling. It was an image of hockey triumph, captured forever in a photo seen around the world.

That season Orr won four individual trophies, including playoff most valuable player (MVP). However, he insisted, "The Stanley Cup is the only trophy I ever wanted."

Next season the Bruins finished first in the league. People expected the team to go all the way. But in the very first round of the playoffs, the Bruins met the Canadiens. Montreal had an untested goalie. Ken Dryden had only played six regular season games. But he helped knock Boston out of the running and wound up guarding the Montreal net for twenty games of postseason play—all the way to the last game in the finals. The Canadiens took the Cup, and Dryden took MVP honors.

Ken Dryden

The Bruins were down but came back. They won the Cup again in 1972, and in 1974 they were back in the finals. This time they faced the Philadelphia Flyers. The Flyers players had nicknames like Moose and Hammer; the owner had signed the toughest, hardest-hitting players he could get. Their star player, Bobby Clarke—considered by many to be a dirty player—was hated by most every opponent. The Flyers won by skill and by fear. Called the "Broad Street Bullies" because of the arena's address, they skated and fought their way to victory against the Bruins, and to the finals the next year, too.

Dave "The Hammer" Schultz

The Flyers had won the first two games against the Buffalo Sabres. But now they were on Sabres home ice. Buffalo was having a warm spell, unusual weather for upstate New York. The game would be unusual, too. It began with a bat, swooping close to the ice, startling the players. Then things got stranger still. By the third period, the temperature in the arena had reached ninety degrees. The ice and heat mixed. A thick fog formed, floating over the rink, making it hard to see the puck. Referees stopped the game twelve

times. Players skated in small circles, trying to break up the fog. Arena workers waved sheets. Nothing worked. Regulation finally ended in a 4–4 tie. In overtime, Sabre René Robert fired a shot at the net. Through the fog, goalie Bernie Parent zeroed in on the puck—a second too late. The Sabres scored and won the game.

The celebration didn't last long. The Flyers took the next two games, along with the Cup.

The Canadiens won the next three trophies. Then, in spring 1979, they faced the Bruins in the semifinals. The series came down to the seventh game. With less than three minutes left in regulation, Boston was ahead 4–3.

All game long, Bruins defender Don Marcotte had shadowed Guy "the Flower" LaFleur, who was the Canadiens' biggest threat. Now, when LaFleur skated to the bench for a breather, Marcotte went out, too. Seconds later, Marcotte exclaimed, "Oh no!" LaFleur was back on the ice. Immediately,

Bruins players jumped in to take Marcotte's place. "Too many! Too many!" yelled the Montreal coach.

Boston had too many men on the ice. The ref called a penalty, probably the most important penalty in hockey history. Now Boston had to play one man down. With little over a minute left, LaFleur scored with a slap shot, about forty feet from the net. Montreal wound up winning the game in overtime, then the series, and the finals, for their fourth championship in a row.

The 1970s closed with a dynasty. And the next decade would bring two more.

CHAPTER 8
Two Dynasties: 1980–1990

By the end of the 1970s, most players wore helmets. There were twenty-one teams in the league. Some were really good teams, such as the Canadiens and the Bruins—and now the New York Islanders. But the Islanders were known as "playoff chokers." They'd never made it to the final round.

All that changed in 1980. Players Bryan Trottier, Mike Bossy, and Denis Potvin began to win—and win big. The team won nineteen playoff series in a row, along with four straight Cups. In 1983, they swept the Edmonton Oilers for the trophy. The Oilers were shocked by the loss. They knew the Islanders had the experience. But the Oilers had the energy, the youth. They thought no one could defeat them. They had the strongest offensive line in the NHL, led by the "Great One"—Wayne Gretzky. But in those games against the Islanders? Gretzky stayed scoreless.

Bryan Trottier of the New York Islanders

Wayne Gretzky (January 26, 1961–)

Considered by many to be the greatest hockey player of all time, Wayne Gretzky, the oldest of five children, practiced for hours on the rink his dad made in their Brantford, Ontario, backyard. By age six he was playing organized hockey with ten-year-olds, and by age ten he was a local celebrity. He signed with the Edmonton Oilers in 1978 and was traded to the Los Angeles Kings in 1988, devastating Edmonton. He was the NHL top scorer every year from 1981 to 1985 and again in 1986–87, and he was named league MVP nine times out of ten from 1980 to 1989. Breaking every major offensive record along the way, Gretzky ended his career with the New York Rangers in 1999.

The Stanley Cup, 1902

The Montreal Victorias were the Stanley Cup champions in 1895.

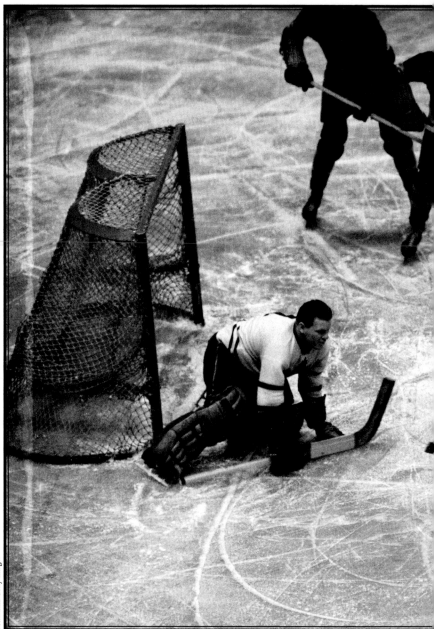

The New York Rangers and Toronto Maple Leafs play
in a Stanley Cup game, 1940.

Montreal Canadiens goalie Jacques Plante blocks a puck, 1955.

Maurice Richard, star of the Montreal Canadiens,
holds the Stanley Cup, 1958.

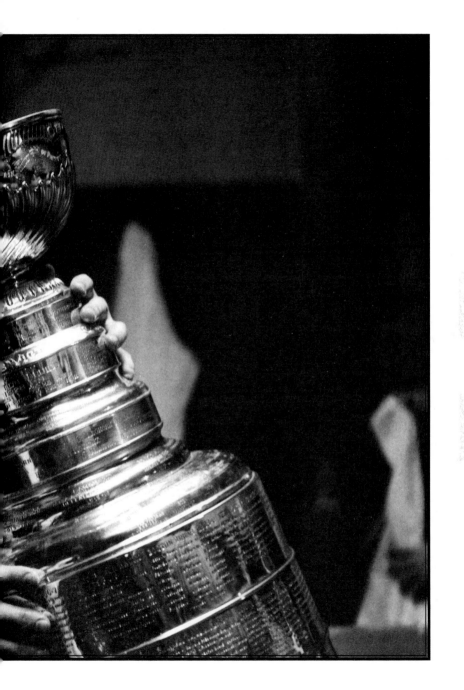

Detroit Red Wings player Gordie Howe

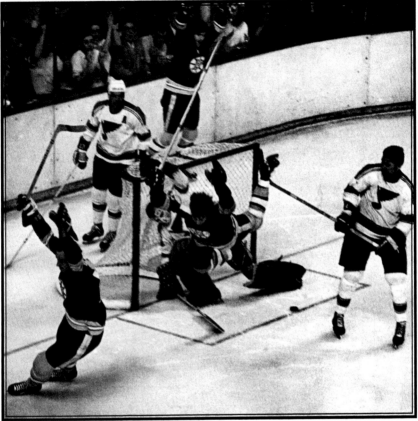

Bobby Orr (center) scores the Stanley Cup–winning goal for the
Boston Bruins, 1970.

Nels Stewart of the Montreal Maroons

Wayne Gretzky playing for the Edmonton Oilers

Washington Capitals player Alex Ovechkin

Mark Messier and other New York Rangers players celebrate their
1994 Stanley Cup win.

After the last game, Gretzky and his teammate, Kevin Lowe, walked past the Islanders' locker room. The men sat quietly, holding ice packs for their injuries. The winners were too tired to celebrate. Lowe told Gretzky, "That's why they won and we didn't. They gave it all they had."

The next year the Oilers made it to the finals, only to face the Islanders again. This time the Oilers gave it all *they* had—and won. In 1985, the Oilers took home the trophy again. And in 1986, they were on track for a three-peat. But in the second round of playoffs against the Calgary Flames, the series stretched to seven games. The deciding game was on April 30, Oiler defender Steve Smith's birthday. With about fifteen minutes left to the game, the score was tied 2–2.

Steve Smith

Players of Color

Grant Fuhr and Willie O'Ree

In 1984, Grant Fuhr became the first player of color to win a Stanley Cup. The first-ever black NHL player, Willie O'Ree, had debuted with the Boston Bruins back in 1958. But diversity has come slowly. Almost eighteen years passed before another black athlete joined the league. In recent years, 93 percent of players have been white. The NHL is looking to increase inclusion with its "Hockey is for Everyone" campaign.

Oiler goalie Grant Fuhr had the puck. He left it behind the net for Smith. Smith quickly retrieved the puck and tried to make a pass. But Fuhr was skating back to the goal. The puck hit his skate, then slid into the net. It was an "own goal" for the Oilers. Upset beyond words, Smith fell to the ice. Calgary won 3–2. The Oilers were out of the Stanley Cup.

Gretzky and his teammates never blamed Smith. They felt it was just one play in the game. The next year, the Oilers rebounded for their third Cup. When Gretzky, as team captain, accepted the trophy, he passed it right to Smith.

Edmonton won again in 1988. This time, Gretzky gathered all the Oilers onto the ice for photos, starting another Cup tradition. Gretzky wanted to treasure the moment. He knew it was his last game with the Oilers.

Gretzky was traded to the Los Angeles Kings for the 1988–89 season. But the Oilers still won the 1990 trophy. Credit should go to the hero of Game 1 of the finals against Boston. The match stretched into three overtimes!

But forward Petr Klima had barely played. He'd been benched for almost three hours—until now. At about 1:30 a.m., fresh off the bench, he led a breakaway to the net. Quickly, he aimed the puck between the goalie's legs. He scored! And the Oilers started the series with a win.

Klima was from Czechoslovakia, which at the time was under the control of the Soviet Union. Five years earlier, he'd sneaked out of a hotel in West Germany during a hockey tournament, met a Red Wings staff member in the woods, then sped away in the dark of night to start his escape. Klima had defected—he'd left his homeland.

As for Gretzky, he watched the last Oilers-Bruins game at home. "I would have liked it to be my team, lifting the Cup," he said. "But these guys were my second choice."

The Soviet Union

After World War I, Russia joined with other countries to form the Soviet Union, a communist country, ruled by one political party. The government owned most businesses, and citizens had few rights. The Soviet Union gained control of neighboring countries, too, like Czechoslovakia and Poland.

And at the end of World War II, an "Iron Curtain" dropped. The term describes the guarded border separating the "Soviet bloc" from the rest of Europe, stopping people from leaving. In 1991, the Soviet Union collapsed.

The Soviet Union and the Iron Curtain, 1950s

SWEDEN

FINLAND

NORWAY

DENMARK

IRELAND

UNITED KINGDOM

NETHERLANDS

EAST GERMANY

POLAND

BELGIUM

WEST GERMANY

CZECHOSLOVAKIA

FRANCE

AUSTRIA

HUNGARY

SWITZ.

ROMANIA

ITALY

YUGOSLAVIA

BULGARIA

PORTUGAL

SPAIN

GREECE

ALBANIA

T

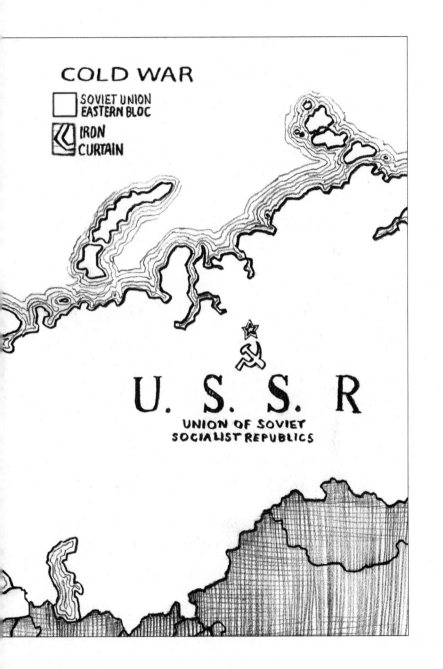

COLD WAR

SOVIET UNION
EASTERN BLOC

IRON
CURTAIN

U. S. S. R

UNION OF SOVIET
SOCIALIST REPUBLICS

CHAPTER 9
A Curse and a Tragedy: 1991–1999

Jaromir Jagr and Mario Lemieux

In the new decade, "Super" Mario Lemieux, and fellow top-scorer Jaromir Jagr, led the Pittsburgh Penguins to back-to-back trophies. Wayne Gretzky had another shot at the title in 1993. But his LA Kings lost to Montreal in the finals.

Meanwhile, Gretzky's old Oilers teammate, Mark Messier, had become captain of the New York Rangers. The Rangers hadn't won the Cup since they had supposedly set it on fire in 1940—fifty-four long years. Now, in the third round of playoffs against the New Jersey Devils, they faced elimination after five games.

"We know we have to win it [Game 6]. We can win it. And we are going to win it," Messier told reporters. Messier wanted to get across to his

teammates how much he believed in them. But his statement was a guarantee. A promise. Now the pressure was really on. Halfway through the game, the Devils were up 2–0. Messier had an assist. The score: 2–1.

Back page of the
New York Post, 1994

Then Messier scored once, twice, three times, to end the game 4–2. He had kept his promise. The Rangers went on to the finals. They were on a roll. But the series, against the Vancouver Canucks, came down to another seventh game. In the stands, Canuck fans chanted, "1940! 1940!" They wanted to remind the Rangers of their curse and their "drought," the many years they'd gone without a championship. It was a tight match. But the Rangers squeaked out a 3–2 win. "The waiting is over!" the television announcer cried.

In 1997, the Detroit Red Wings ended their own forty-two-year drought, thanks to the famous "Russian Five." The Soviet Union had collapsed in 1991 and now, for the first time, Russians could easily join the NHL. That's exactly what these five men had done.

Back row: Vladimir Konstantinov, Sergei Fedorov, and Vyncheslav Fetisov
Front row: Slava Kozlov and Igor Larionov

Six days after the victory, the Red Wings celebrated with a golf outing. Star defender Vladimir Konstantinov, one of the Russian Five, climbed into a limousine with two friends. Minutes later, the driver lost control. The limo slammed into a tree. One teammate had minor injuries. Konstantinov and the team trainer had survived but were in comas, unconscious.

Konstantinov was a fan favorite. Nicknamed the "Vladinator," after the Terminator movie character, he had his own pregame video of hard-hitting plays. But to his teammates, Konstantinov, with his goofy grin, seemed more like Curious George. After the accident, it took months for Konstantivov just to learn to walk again. And with severe head injuries, he'd never be the same.

The Red Wings dedicated their next season to the injured men. They wore patches on their uniforms in English and Russian that said "Believe." And they made it to the finals. Konstantinov was in a wheelchair, sitting in the stands for the deciding game.  When Detroit swept the Washington Capitals, he was brought onto the ice for the trophy presentation. Captain Steve Yzerman didn't lift the Cup. He passed it straight to Konstantinov. The entire team huddled around the ex-player in friendship and support.

No Detroit player has worn his number since.

CHAPTER 10
Legends, Old and New: 2000–2018

In 2000, Bruins star Raymond Bourque became part of the Colorado Avalanche. Bourque had played twenty-one seasons for Boston. He'd been a strong and steady leader and an all-around nice guy, with five trophies for Best Defender. He'd led his team to two finals. But he'd never won a Cup. Now, thirty-nine years old and about

to retire, he wanted it more than ever. So at his request, Boston traded him to Colorado. For Bourque, it was a gut-wrenching decision.

Boston couldn't make the playoffs. And the

Raymond Bourque

Avalanche had a good chance of going all the way. But then Colorado was knocked out in the semifinals.

At the beginning of the next season, Captain Joe Sakic told Bourque, "We're going to win. And I want you to be the first to lift the Cup." The entire team got behind Bourque. They called their mission "16W," for the sixteen playoff wins needed for Bourque to retire a champion. This time, the Avalanche made it to the finals. In Game 3 against the Devils, Bourque scored the winning goal. But the series went to a seventh

game. Bourque played most of it. "They wanted me there right to the end," he said. As the clock ticked down, it became clear the Avalanche would win. Still on the ice, Bourque held back tears.

The buzzer sounded. The game was over. Cries of "Ray! Ray!" rocked the arena. Five days later, Bourque came back to Boston. He stood by City Hall in front of fifteen thousand loyal fans. "This is home for me and my family," he said.

Smiling, Bourque lifted the trophy for all to share his joy.

The Red Wings, Devils, and Tampa Bay Lightning won the next three championships. But the entire 2004–05 season was canceled. Owners and players couldn't agree on contracts. For the first time ever, there was no championship series. But hockey was back in action the next season, with rookies Sidney Crosby and Alex Ovechkin; Crosby skating for the Penguins, Ovechkin for the Capitals. The next year, nineteen-year-old Crosby took the scoring title, the youngest player ever to win that trophy. In 2009, at twenty-one, he was the youngest captain to take his team to Stanley Cup victory.

Alex Ovechkin

Sidney Crosby (August 7, 1987–)

Sidney Crosby and his younger sister grew up outside Halifax, Nova Scotia. Their father, Troy, was a hockey player, drafted by the Canadiens, and

the family's basement became a makeshift rink. At age fifteen, Crosby went to a boarding school in Minnesota known for its hockey program and led his team to a national title. Back in Canada, he entered the 2005 NHL draft, known by fans as "The Sidney Crosby Sweepstakes." Plagued by concussions over the years, Crosby still managed to win top scoring trophies.

Meanwhile, Chicago fans hoped 2010 would be the year of the Blackhawks. They'd only won three championships since the team began playing in 1926. The finals against Philadelphia could end their drought. And Game 6 could be the clincher. In overtime, Hawks forward Patrick Kane tried to shake a Flyer defender. It seemed impossible. Together, they skated closer to the net. Somehow Kane fired a quick shot on goal. There were no cheers, no red light signaling he scored. No one knew what happened, although Kane skated away, shouting in triumph.

Patrick Kane

But did the puck really go in? Replays show it did. Kane's shot had won the game and the Cup! The puck had slid into the padding at the bottom of the net and disappeared from sight. Immediately, it became the most famous puck in Chicago history. Unfortunately, no one could find it after the game. Newspapers ran the story of the missing puck. A restaurant owner offered a $50,000 reward. Nobody came forward. What happened to the mysterious puck? Chicago fans are still waiting to find out.

In 2012, the Kings made headlines. They didn't have a great season. They were the lowest-ranked team to make the playoffs. But they took it one game at a time, knocking out team after team. In the deciding game of the finals, they blew out the Devils 6–1.

The Kings became the first "worst" team to win a championship. Meanwhile, the Hawks still had momentum, winning Cups in 2013 and 2015. Crosby and the Penguins followed in 2016. If they won in 2017, they'd be the first team since 1998 to win back-to-back championships. If the Nashville Predators won, it would be their first championship—period.

At their home arena, Predator fans tossed catfish—a Nashville favorite food—onto the ice, just as they'd been doing since 2002. Most likely, a fan had been inspired by the Red Wings' "fishy" tradition. Back in 1952, two brothers tossed an octopus into the Detroit rink. The octopus had eight arms, and the team needed eight playoff wins

to take the trophy. It seemed to make sense. (In fact, hockey has a history of fans tossing objects onto the ice: hats after hat tricks, hamburgers for goalie Andrew "the Hamburglar" Hammond, and small leopard sharks for the San Jose Sharks, to name a few.)

Andrew "the Hamburglar" Hammond

The octopus had worked for Detroit in 1952. They won the title. Would catfish do the same for Nashville? In Game 6, the Penguins had the chance to win it all. But the Predators fought back. The first period ended in a 0–0 tie. In the second period, Nashville's Colton Sisson shot a rebound into the goal. Were the Predators and their catfish-loving fans on the way to victory?

No! The referee had already blown his whistle for play to stop, thinking the goalie had the puck. In the noisy arena, no one had heard it. It was an iffy call. But it couldn't be changed. The Predators didn't recover, and the Penguins went on to score twice. They won the game, the series, and the trophy.

Would Crosby take his team to more finals, more Stanley Cup wins? Or would he be overshadowed by Alex Ovechkin? Ovechkin is considered the greatest scorer of his generation, and in 2018, his Capitals were hungry for a trophy. The team had come close before but never won, losing time and again to Pittsburgh in the postseason.

This time Washington came out on top in the second round, then battled their way to the finals. They faced a surprise opponent: the newest team to join the NHL, the Vegas Golden Knights. After losing the first game, the Capitals took the next four matches—and the title.

But maybe, with more experience under their team belt, the Golden Knights will make another appearance in the Stanley Cup championship. Maybe that series will go to the last possible game . . . to the last possible second . . . into overtime and beyond.

You never know what could happen in a Stanley Cup game.

Timeline of the Stanley Cup

1875 — James Creighton organizes the first indoor hockey game in Montreal, with official rules and a puck

1893 — The first Stanley Cup champion is crowned, the Montreal Hockey Club

1914 — "World Series of Hockey" era begins with East/West championship

1917 — The first US team, the Seattle Metropolitans, wins the Cup

1919 — The series is canceled due to Spanish flu epidemic

1936 — Detroit Red Wings defeat the Montreal Maroons in the longest game in playoff history

1942 — The Original Six era begins

1944 — Montreal Canadien Maurice "Rocket" Richard scores all five goals against Toronto in the semifinals, tying the record for an NHL playoff game

1974 — Philadelphia Flyers take the Stanley Cup, becoming the first NHL expansion team to win the title

1979 — Boston Bruins lose to Montreal in the finals, after taking a penalty for too many men on the ice

1984 — The Edmonton Oilers begin a dynasty with their first Cup win

2005 — No Stanley Cup played; owners and players fight about money and the season is canceled

2009 — At twenty-one, Pittsburgh Penguins star Sidney Crosby becomes the youngest captain to lead a team to the Stanley Cup

Timeline of the World

1876 — Alexander Graham Bell makes the first successful phone call

1892 — New York's major immigration entryway, Ellis Island, opens

1893 — New Zealand becomes the first self-governing nation to grant all women the right to vote

1917 — On April 6, the United States enters World War I

1919 — After a storage tank bursts, more than two million gallons of syrup sweep Boston streets, killing twenty-one people

1927 — Charles Lindbergh flies from New York to Paris in the first nonstop solo flight across the Atlantic

1936 — Nazi dictator Adolf Hitler opens the Summer Olympic Games in Berlin

1942 — The United States defeats Japan in the Battle of Midway, a turning point in World War II

1974 — US president Richard Nixon resigns on August 8

1979 — Sony unveils the Walkman, the first personal music device to play cassettes

1984 — An American chemical plant in Bhopal, India, leaks, killing fifteen thousand people in one of the world's worst industrial disasters

2005 — Hurricane Katrina strikes the US Gulf Coast in August

2009 — Barack Obama becomes the first African American US president

Bibliography

*Books for young readers

Allen, Kevin. *"Then Wayne Said to Mario . . ." The Best Stanley Cup Stories Ever Told*. Chicago: Triumph Books, 2009.

Diamond, Dan, James Duplacey, and Eric Zweig. *The Ultimate Prize: The Stanley Cup*. Kansas City: Andrews McMeel Publishing, 2003.

Falla, Jack, general editor. *Quest for the Cup: A History of the Stanley Cup Finals 1893–2001*. Toronto: Key Porter Books, 2001.

*Zweig, Eric. *Hockey Trivia for Kids 3: Stanley Cup Edition*. Toronto: Scholastic Canada, 2011.

Zweig, Eric. *Stanley Cup: 120 Years of Hockey Supremacy*. Buffalo, NY, and Richmond Hill, Ontario: Firefly Books, 2012.